AFFILIATE MARKETING

SECRET

FOR BEGINNERS

How to Make a Fortune Online

Without a Product of Your Own

AMOS D. JOHNSON

All rights reserved. No part of this publication may be reproduced, distributed, or transmitted in any form or by any means, including photocopying, recording, or other electronic or mechanical methods, without the prior written permission of the publisher, except in the case of brief quotations embodied in critical reviews and certain other noncommercial uses permitted by copyright law.

Copyright © Amos D. Johnson, 2024.

ABOUT THE AUTHOR

"Amos D. Johnson is a highly successful affiliate marketer and online entrepreneur with a passion for helping others succeed in the digital space. With over a decade of experience in the industry, Amos has built a reputation for his expertise in driving sales, generating leads, and creating successful online businesses.

Through his own journey, Amos has learned the secrets to success in affiliate marketing and has helped countless individuals achieve their financial goals. He is dedicated to sharing his knowledge and insights with beginners, providing a clear and comprehensive guide to getting started with affiliate marketing. Amos's approach is centered around simplicity, clarity, and actionable strategies that anyone can apply. His goal is to empower readers with the skills and confidence they need to succeed in affiliate marketing and build a profitable online business.

In this book, Affiliate Marketing Secrets for Beginners, Amos shares his expertise and reveals the secrets to success in affiliate marketing, providing a step-by-step guide for those just starting out."

TABLE OF CONTENT

CHAPTER 1 11

    WHAT IS AFFILIATE MARKETING? 11

    HOW AFFILIATE MARKETING WORKS 14

    BENEFITS OF AFFILIATE MARKETING 15

CHAPTER 2 21

    UNDERSTANDING AFFILIATES NETWORKING 21

CHAPTER 3 25

    FINDING A NICHE 25

    SETTING UP YOUR ONLINE PRESENCE 28

CHAPTER 4 35

    RESEARCHING AFFILIATE PROGRAMS 35

    CHOOSING A PRODUCT TO ADVERTISE 40

CHAPTER 5 45

    EFFECTIVE PRODUCT REVIEWS 45

CHAPTER 6 51

    CREATING AN EMAIL LIST 51

    SOCIAL MEDIA MARKETING FOR AFFILIATES 55

CHAPTER 7 59

    CONTENT MARKETING STRATEGIES 59

CHAPTER 8 65

    OPTIMIZING YOUR WEBSITE FOR CONVERSION 65

    USING PAID ADVERTISING TO SUPERCHARGE YOUR AFFILIATE MARKETING 70

CHAPTER 9 75

    BUILDING A TEAM AND OUTSOURCING TASKS - BECAUSE YOU CAN'T DO IT ALONE! 75

UNDERSTANDING AFFILIATE TRACKING AND ANALYTICS - THE SECRET TO MAXIMIZING YOUR EARNINGS!...................80

CHAPTER 10 85

THE KEY TO EXPLODING YOUR PROFITS: MAXIMIZING YOUR CAMPAIGN FOR MAXIMUM PROFIT 85

AVOID AFFILIATE MARKETING MISTAKES - DON'T LET THESE COMMON PITFALLS HOLD YOU BACK!...89

CHAPTER 1

WHAT IS AFFILIATE MARKETING?

A Form of internet marketing known as affiliate marketing is promoting goods or services from another business in exchange for a commission on purchases or referrals made using your special affiliate link.

Say a buddy tells you about a fantastic new restaurant they just tried while you're at a dinner party. You choose to test the restaurant because you believe what your buddy has to say. If the cuisine is good, you may recommend it to your friends, who could then visit as well. The restaurant is comparable to a product or service in affiliate marketing, and your buddy is comparable to an affiliate marketer. When you purchase the product that the affiliate marketer has recommended to you, they will get a commission.

FOR INTANCE:

Assume you run a well-known fitness blog and collaborate with a firm that offers exercise gear. You evaluate their new treadmill and provide a link to their website so readers may purchase the item. You will get a commission on sales made if one of your readers clicks on the link and purchases the treadmill.

Here's an illustration of how this might function:

-By enrolling in the exercise equipment company's affiliate network, you may monitor your referrals using a special affiliate link.

- You provide an evaluation of the treadmill along with your affiliate link on your blog.

- A reader of yours clicks the link and spends $1,000 on the treadmill.

- A $100 commission, or 10% of the sale, is yours.

In this instance, you have earned a commission by promoting a product that you believe in. Your reader receives a fantastic product, and the business gains from more visibility and revenue. A win-win-win situation exists!

HOW AFFILIATE MARKETING WORKS

1. An advertiser (the company selling the product) partners with an affiliate network or creates their own in-house affiliate program.

2. After enrolling in the affiliate program, you, the affiliate marketer, get a special affiliate link or code that allows you to monitor referrals.

3. Using a variety of marketing channels, you tell your audience about the product (social media, blog articles, email marketing, etc.).

4. You are paid a commission when a customer uses your affiliate link to purchase the item.

A common strategy used by people and companies to monetize their internet presence and promote goods they support is affiliate marketing. Because it's a performance-based marketing approach, you only get paid when a customer purchases the item or fulfills a goal.

BENEFITS OF AFFILIATE MARKETING

There are several advantages to affiliate marketing for both marketers and affiliates. The following are some of the main benefits:

1. Minimal Risk: Since you only pay for outcomes, launching an affiliate marketing program is comparatively risk-free (i.e., sales or referrals).

For instance, as an advertiser, you don't have to worry about shelling out cash for promotional items or ad space that may not bring in any business. You only get paid when a customer purchases your item or service.

2. Broader Reach: By connecting you with a large network of affiliates, you may reach a wider audience and get more exposure for your items.

For instance, if your business sells exercise equipment, collaborating with bloggers and fitness influencers might help you expand your market and build brand recognition.

3. Cost-Effective: Compared to conventional advertising tactics like print or TV commercials, affiliate marketing is a cost-effective approach to promote your items since you only pay for real sales or referrals.

As an example, you don't have to pay for marketing materials or advertising when you're an affiliate marketer pushing a product. Only when a customer purchases the item via your special affiliate link do you get paid?

4. Flexibility: Affiliate marketing is a great choice for anyone who wants to work remotely or has a flexible schedule since it can be done from any location with an internet connection.

Example: Affiliate marketing may be a terrific method to make money while still having the freedom to take care of your family or travel whether you're a stay-at-home parent or a digital nomad.

5. Passive revenue: As long as customers keep purchasing things using your affiliate link after you've set up your affiliate marketing campaign, you may get passive revenue.

Example: Even if you're not actively marketing the online course, you may still make money as an affiliate marketer if someone purchases it using your affiliate link.

6. Minimal Overhead: Since you won't have to worry about inventory, shipping, or customer service, starting an affiliate marketing business will cost you very little in overhead.

As an example, as an advertiser, you are relieved of the burden of product storage and shipment; it is the responsibility of the affiliate marketer.

7. Data-Driven Insights: By offering useful information and insights on customer behavior, affiliate marketing enables you to enhance your marketing plans and merchandise.

As an example, affiliate marketing data may be used by advertisers to determine which goods are selling well, which target audiences are most interested in your offerings, and other information.

8. Develop credibility: When your target audience sees that other individuals are endorsing your items, working with affiliates may assist in cultivating trust and credibility with them.

For instance, if your business is young, collaborating with well-established affiliates might help you get the respect and confidence of your target market.

In conclusion, affiliate marketing provides a flexible, low-risk, and affordable means to advertise goods and make money. It also can generate passive revenue and provide insightful data.

CHAPTER 2

UNDERSTANDING AFFILIATES NETWORKING

The foundation of affiliate marketing is provided by affiliate networks, which link advertisers and affiliates and provide the tools needed to monitor and manage affiliate campaigns. We'll dive into the world of affiliate networks in this part, explaining what they are, how they operate, and what advantages they provide.

What is an Affiliate Network?

An affiliate network is a platform that links publications that promote a merchant's goods or services with marketers (sometimes referred to as advertisers). Serving as a middleman, the network offers a marketplace where marketers can locate affiliates and affiliates can discover items to promote.

How Do Networks of Affiliates Operate?

This is a detailed explanation of how affiliate networks operate:

1. Marketers sign up for the network and establish affiliate schemes for their goods or services.

2. After connecting with the network, affiliates seek to become part of the advertiser's affiliate program.

3. Upon approval, affiliates have access to special affiliate IDs that allow them to monitor the

referrals they make as well as marketing materials like banners, links, and product feeds.

4. Using a variety of marketing platforms (such as social media, email marketing, and blog postings), affiliates market the advertiser's goods and services.

5. The network keeps track of sales made by customers who click on an affiliate's link and pay the affiliate a commission.

6. The network processes payments, making sure that affiliates are paid the commissions they have earned.

Benefits of Network Affiliates

There are many advantages that affiliate networks provide to both marketers and affiliates:

- **Convenience**: Affiliates have access to a vast marketplace of items to promote, and advertisers may oversee several affiliate programs from a single platform.

- **Tracking and Reporting**: Networks provide comprehensive reporting and tracking features that make it simple to keep an eye on campaign effectiveness and performance.

- Payment processing is handled by networks, which guarantees accurate and timely commission payouts.

- **Support:** To ensure the success of its affiliates, several networks provide community forums and training.

CHAPTER 3

FINDING A NICHE

In affiliate marketing, picking a lucrative product or services is essential. A niche is a particular interest or target market to which you will direct your product promotion efforts. Your affiliate marketing success may be determined by selecting the appropriate niche.

Why Is It Important to Choose a Niche?

1. **Targeted audience**: By using a niche, you may more effectively reach a certain audience and increase the chance that they will become clients.

2. Relevant products: By concentrating on a certain niche, you may advertise goods that are pertinent to the requirements and preferences of your target market.

3. Less competition: By focusing on a certain specialty, you may stand out from the crowd and get attention.

4. Authority building: By focusing on a certain area of knowledge, you may gain the audience's confidence by demonstrating your authority.

How Do I Pick a Lucrative Niche?

1. Determine your interests: To begin, jot down your interests, passions, and areas of specialization.

2. Do market research: Look into well-known industries such as technology, finance, and health and wellness.

3. Examine the competition: To examine the competition and demand, use tools such as Google Trends, Keyword Tool, or SEMrush.

4. Assess profitability: Make sure the items and affiliate programs in your selected category have competitive commissions by researching them.

5. Verify demand: To verify interest and demand in your selected topic, use Google searches, social media, and online forums.

SETTING UP YOUR ONLINE PRESENCE

For affiliate marketers, having a strong online presence is essential. It enables you to efficiently market your items, expand your audience, and establish a reputation.

-Select a Domain for a Specific Niche

Choose a domain name that accurately represents your brand or expertise. This will assist you in creating a credible online persona.

As an example, if fitness is your niche, register a domain name such as (link unavailable) or (link unavailable).

-Pick a Trustworthy Web Hosting Provider

Select a web hosting provider that provides scalability, excellent customer care, and dependable uptime.

For instance, well-known web hosts Bluehost, SiteGround, and HostGator provide dependable uptime and excellent customer service.

-Install an application for content management (CMS)

Use a content management system (CMS) like WordPress, Joomla, or Drupal to simply manage the content of your website.

Example: With a large selection of themes, plugins, and customization possibilities, WordPress is a well-liked content management system.

-Create a Responsive Website

Make a website that is aesthetically pleasing, mobile-device and responsive.

Example: To develop a responsive website that looks amazing on desktop and mobile devices, choose a website builder such as Divi, Beaver Builder, or Elementor.

-Produce Useful Content

Create a content plan that includes valuable stuff for your audience, such as podcasts, videos, and blog articles. Make a video like "How to Do a Perfect Squat" or a blog piece like "10 Tips for Starting a Home Workout Routine" as an example.

-Create an Account on Social Media

Make accounts on pertinent social media networks and interact with users.

As an example, set up a Twitter handle, Instagram account, or Facebook page to engage with your followers and distribute your work.

-Create an Email List: Install an email marketing platform to draw in subscribers and provide them with insightful information.

As an example, use an email marketing platform like Mailchimp or ConvertKit to gather subscribers and nurture them with periodic newsletters or sales emails.

-Set up necessary tools and plugins

To improve the functionality of your website, add plugins and utilities like affiliate link management, security, and SEO optimization.

Example: To manage your affiliate links, protect your website from malware, and optimize it for search engines, use plugins like Yoast SEO, Wordfence Security, or Affiliate Links.

-Make search engine optimizations

Make sure your website is search engine optimized to increase exposure and attract natural visitors.

For instance, to optimize your website for search engines, use phrases like "fitness tips," "home workout routine," or "weight loss advice."

-Track and Examine Results

Utilize analytics tools to monitor the effectiveness of your website, get insight into your target audience, and make informed choices.

Example: Monitor the traffic, engagement, and conversion rates of your website using analytics programs like Jetpack or Google Analytics.

You may create a polished online presence that draws in and interacts with your target audience and facilitates your success in affiliate marketing by following these steps.

CHAPTER 4

RESEARCHING AFFILIATE PROGRAMS

Your success as an affiliate marketer depends on selecting the appropriate affiliate program. This is a detailed how-to for investigating affiliate programs:

1. Identify Your Niche: Decide on your specialty and the goods or services you want to advertise. For instance, if you run a fitness blog, your area of expertise may be exercise supplements or fitness gear.

2. Look into Affiliate Networks Examine well-known affiliate networks such as Commission Junction, ShareASale, ClickBank, and Amazon Associates.

For instance, you may sign up for the ShareASale network, which has many fitness goods, or the Amazon Associates program if you want to market exercise equipment.

3. Look for Affiliate Programs: To identify affiliate programs relevant to your specialty, use search engines or affiliate network directories.

For instance, to uncover relevant possibilities, search for "fitness affiliate programs" or "workout supplement affiliate programs."

4. Review Program conditions: Take a look at the minimum payout amounts, commission rates, cookie lengths, and payment conditions of the program.

Example: There is a minimum payment requirement of $10 and a 24-hour cookie length when you sign up for the Amazon Associates program. You will get a 4-6% reward on purchases.

5. Do your research on the product or service to make sure it is reputable, of excellent quality, and relevant to your target market.

For instance, if you want to advertise a supplement for exercise, be sure your audience would benefit from it by reading the product's ratings, reviews, and components.

6. **Affiliate assistance:** Seek programs that provide marketing materials, training materials, and specialized affiliate assistance.

For instance, to assist you in succeeding, several affiliate programs include seminars, email assistance, or even a personal affiliate manager.

7. Read Affiliate Agreements: Before joining, make sure you are aware of the terms and circumstances of the affiliate agreement.

Example: Be sure you are aware of the expectations placed on you as an affiliate and the guidelines you must adhere to while endorsing goods.

8. Test and Promote: To make sure the product or service converts properly, test it and then market it to your target.

Example: To foster trust and boost sales, try out a supplement for exercise yourself and then tell your audience about your experience.

Some popular affiliate programs to consider:

- Amazon Associates

- ShareASale

- ClickBank

- Commission Junction

- Rakuten

- eBay Partner Network

- Target Affiliates

- Walmart Affiliates

Recall that doing extensive research on affiliate programs will enable you to optimize your profits and choose the ideal match for your audience.

CHOOSING A PRODUCT TO ADVERTISE

As an affiliate marketer, choosing the appropriate product to promote is essential to your success. Here's a detailed guide to help you choose a product:

1. **Align with Your Niche:** Choose a Product That Fits Your Expertise or Niche.

2. **Investigate Well-Known items:** To locate well-known items, use internet resources including social media, Google Trends, and Amazon Best Sellers.

3. **Assess goods Quality:** Make sure the goods are well-made, timely, and reputable.

4. **Review the Affiliate Program conditions:** Confirm the commission rates, cookie lengths, and conditions of payment of the affiliate program.

5. Analyze the Competition: Evaluate how the competitors are marketing the product and look for ways to differentiate yourself.

6. Examine Product Reviews: Make sure the product satisfies the demands of your audience by reading customer reviews and ratings.

7. Test the Product: Give the product a try to make sure it lives up to your expectations and to gain the audience's confidence.

8. Assess Vendor assistance: Make sure the vendor provides resources, marketing materials, and dependable assistance.

9. Take into Account the Product's Price Point: Select a product whose price point fits the means and willingness to pay off your target audience.

10. Seek for items with Recurring Commissions: To increase your profits, advertise items that have recurring commissions.

11. Assess the Product's Sales Page: Make sure the page is compelling, well-designed, and simple to use.

12. Look for Any Other Income Streams: Search for items that provide extra revenue opportunities like cross- or up-selling.

Some popular product to consider:

- Digital product (such as software, e-books, and courses).

-Tangible product (e.g., gadgets, supplements, workout equipment)

-Services (such as web hosting, virtual education, and consultancy)

You may choose a product that appeals to your audience and optimizes your affiliate income by following these steps.

Additional tips:

-Suggest items that your audience needs or solves problems with; -Select products from reliable suppliers that have a solid track record of paying affiliates

To boost conversions, think about offering items with a free demo or trial.

- To safeguard your affiliate links and boost click-through rates, use affiliate link cloaking solutions. - To establish credibility with your audience, reveal your relationship to the product provider.

CHAPTER 5

EFFECTIVE PRODUCT REVIEWS

An essential component of affiliate marketing is product evaluations, which assist your audience in making knowledgeable purchases. Here's a how-to manual for writing persuasive product reviews:

1. Make use of an attention-grabbing title: Write a headline that both draws the reader in and appropriately summarizes the substance of your review.

2. Give a brief description of the product: Give a brief description of the product, including its features, advantages, and intended market.

3. Share your own experience: Talk about how you utilized the product and what you liked and didn't like about it.

4. Emphasize the product's features: List the main attributes of the product and explain how they help the consumer.

5. List the benefits and drawbacks of the product to provide a fair assessment of it.

6. Make use of visuals: Provide screenshots, movies, or photographs that highlight the benefits of the product and your use of it.

7. Compare with comparable items: draw attention to the product's special qualities and advantages while contrasting it with comparable products on the market.

8. **Incorporate a call-to-action (CTA):** Use a button or link to nudge readers to take action.

9. **Disclose your affiliation:** To gain the audience's confidence, disclose your relationship with the product provider.

10. **SEO Optimization**: Use relevant keywords, meta descriptions, and picture optimization to make your review more search engine friendly.

For instance:

Headline: "Fitness Tracker Review: Does it Work?"

Summary: "In this review, I'll be sharing my experience with the XYZ Fitness Tracker, a popular choice among fitness enthusiasts."

My own experience: "I used the fitness tracker for a month and found it to be incredibly useful in tracking my daily activity and progress."

Specifications: "The fitness tracker features a heart rate monitor, GPS tracking, and water resistance up to 50 meters."

Advantages and disadvantages:

- Positives: "Accurate tracking, comfortable design, and long battery life."

- Negatives: "Limited compatibility with certain devices, no built-in GPS."

Illustrations: "Here's a screenshot of the fitness tracker's dashboard, showing my daily activity and progress."

Contrast: "Compared to similar products in the market, the XYZ Fitness Tracker offers more features at an affordable price."

Instructions for action: "Get your XYZ Fitness Tracker today and start tracking your fitness journey!"

Disclaimer: "Note: I am an affiliate of the XYZ Fitness Tracker and earn a commission for each sale made through my unique referral link."

These guidelines will help you write insightful product evaluations that both assist your audience in making wise purchases and boost your affiliate income.

CHAPTER 6

CREATING AN EMAIL LIST

An essential first step in affiliate marketing is creating an email list, which enables you to offer items and cultivate a connection with your audience. Here's how to create an email list step-by-step:

1. Select an ESP (email service provider): To handle your email list, use a reputable ESP such as AWeber, ConvertKit, or Mailchimp.

2. Make a Lead Magnet: To get people to sign up for your list, provide a useful resource (such as an eBook, webinar, or checklist).

3. Design an Opt-in Form: Make an eye-catching opt-in form and post it on your website or landing page to collect email addresses.

4. Drive Traffic to Your Opt-in Form: To increase traffic to your opt-in form, use paid advertising, content marketing, and social media.

5. Create Captivating Email Content: Write email content that captivates readers and fosters confidence.

6. Segment Your Email List: To boost engagement and conversions, segment your list according to demographics or hobbies.

7. Make Use of Email Automation: Create automated email campaigns to market your goods and nurture leads.

8. Adhere to Email Marketing Regulations: To stay out of trouble with the law, make sure you abide by rules like CAN-SPAM and GDPR.

For instance:

"Download the Ultimate Fitness Guide" is the lead magnet.

"Enter your email address to get instant access" is the opt-in form.

Email Body: "Hey [Name], thank you for joining our fitness community! Obtain exclusive advice and discounts.

"Health Professionals" and "Fitness Enthusiasts" portions

Automation: "Abandoned cart" and "Welcome series"

You may enhance your affiliate revenue and create a focused email list by following these steps.

Additional Tips;

- Make your subject line succinct and precise.

Make use of a prominent and compelling call-to-action (CTA) button.

Make use of social evidence, such as endorsements or trust seals

Make your design mobile-friendly.

- To secure consent, use a twofold opt-in procedure.

- Implement an understandable and open privacy policy

SOCIAL MEDIA MARKETING FOR AFFILIATES

Affiliates may promote items, establish connections, and reach a larger audience with the use of social media marketing. This is an affiliates' step-by-step guide for social media marketing:

1. Select the Correct Platforms: Pay attention to social media sites like Facebook, Instagram, Twitter, and LinkedIn where your target market is most engaged.

2. Produce Interesting Content: Post insightful articles, such as product evaluations, how-to guides, or business news that your audience finds interesting.

3. Make Use of Visuals: To set your material apart, use eye-catching pictures, videos, or infographics.

4. Make Use of Hashtags: To improve exposure and connect with more people, use pertinent hashtags.

5. Work Together with Influencers: To increase your exposure and reputation, collaborate with influencers in your area.

6. Run Social Media Ads: To target certain audiences and increase traffic to your affiliate link, use paid advertising.

7. Disseminate User-Generated Content: Invite your customers to write about their product experiences, then repost them on your social media pages.

8. Make utilize of Affiliate Links: To safeguard your commissions, post your affiliate link on social media and utilize affiliate link cloaking software.

9. Watch and Participate: Give prompt, tailored responses to remarks, messages, and mentions.

10. Monitor Your Outcomes: Make necessary adjustments to your approach based on the effectiveness of your social media efforts by using analytics tools.

For instance:

Assume you are an affiliate marketer who uses Twitter to advertise a well-liked e-book reader. You make a tweet that highlights the advantages of the e-reader and includes a picture of someone using it to read an e-book. You tag the official account of the e-book reader and include pertinent hashtags, such as #e-books #reading #tech. In addition, you provide a video evaluation of the gadget and invite your fans to recommend e-books to you.

You may use social media to market items, cultivate connections, and boost your affiliate income by following these guidelines.

Additional Tips:

-To make content scheduling and sharing more efficient, use social media management tools like Hoot suite or Buffer. - For behind-the-scenes material and exclusive promos, use Instagram Stories and Facebook Live.

Use social media tools designed specifically for affiliate marketing, such as Affiliate Link Cloaker or Social Share Locker. - Make a social media content calendar to plan and arrange your content ahead of time. - Declare your affiliation with the product vendor on your social media posts to foster transparency and trust.

CHAPTER 7

CONTENT MARKETING STRATEGIES

Affiliates may use content marketing as a potent tool to draw in and interact with their target audience, establish credibility and trust, and eventually increase revenue. The following are some successful affiliate content marketing techniques:

1. Provide Useful and Relevant Material: Provide material that speaks to the needs, passions, and problems of your audience. Posts on social media, podcasts, videos, blogs, and more may all fall under this category.

For instance, if you're marketing a financial planning tool, make content like "10 Tips for Saving Money on a Tight Budget" or "How to Create a Budget That Works" that tackles typical financial issues.

2. Use a Content Calendar: Make use of a content calendar to plan and arrange your material ahead of time. By doing this, you can guarantee efficiency, consistency, and harmony with your marketing objectives.

Make a monthly content calendar, for instance, including the subjects, styles, and deadlines for your articles. As an example, you may schedule the release of a video on the eighth and twenty-second of every month and a blog article on the first and fifteenth.

3. Make Use of User-Generated Content: Invite people in your audience to write and publish articles on your affiliated goods or services. This may contain reviews, images, videos, and testimonies from customers.

For instance, hold a social media competition whereby participants are asked to use a certain hashtag to post their best money-saving or money-management strategies. After that, you may repost this information on your social media platforms, making sure to give credit to the original authors.

4. Make Use of Email Marketing: To share your content, advertise your affiliate product, grow your audience, establish an email list, and send out newsletters or promotional emails regularly.

Example: Include a call-to-action to visit your affiliate link in your weekly email, along with a link to your most recent blog article and a special offer or discount.

5. Work with Influencers: To increase your audience engagement, reputation, and reach, collaborate with influencers in your field.

For instance, get in touch with a well-known personal finance writer and inquire about working together on a blog post or social media series that highlights your affiliate product.

6. Optimize for Search Engines: Make sure your material is search engine optimized to raise your affiliate profits, enhance exposure, and attract organic visitors.

For instance, to draw in relevant search engine traffic, use keywords such as "best budgeting apps" or "how to invest in stocks" in the headers, meta descriptions, and titles of your blog posts.

7. Repurpose and Update Content: Give your current content a fresh start by adapting it to new forms, target audiences, or distribution channels.

Example: Update an old article with new material and republish it, or turn a well-liked blog piece into a video or social media series.

By putting these content marketing methods into practice, you'll be able to draw in and interact with your target audience, establish credibility and trust, and eventually boost sales and affiliate income.

Additional Tips;

- Speak conversationally and emphasize advantages over features.

- Make use of captivating images and _mobile-friendly_

- Promote interaction via email replies, social media shares, and comments.

Make use of content tools tailored to affiliate marketing, such as Affiliate Link Cloaker or Content Egg.

- To foster trust and openness, clearly state in your article that you are not affiliated with the product seller.

CHAPTER 8

OPTIMIZING YOUR WEBSITE FOR CONVERSION

To get the most out of your affiliate marketing campaigns, you must optimize your website for conversions. Having a website that is both aesthetically pleasing and easy to use may greatly increase the likelihood that users will click on your affiliate links and complete a transaction. The following techniques may help you improve your website for conversions:

1. Content that is Clear and Concise: Make sure the information on your website is relevant to your target, clear, and concise. Make your writing basic and divide lengthy paragraphs into manageable chunks.

2. Prominent Affiliate Links: Place your affiliate links in a visible place on your website, particularly on instructional or product review pages. Make use of attention-grabbing banners or buttons.

3. Product Reviews and Ratings: To establish credibility and trust, provide consumer ratings and reviews of your products. This may make it more likely that users will click on your affiliate links.

4. Visuals and photos: To highlight goods and improve the readability of your material, use excellent visuals and photos. This may improve visitors' comprehension of the merchandise and boost conversion rates.

5. Streamlined Navigation: Make sure the navigation on your website is simple to use and streamlined. Make it easy for people to click on your affiliate links and locate what they're searching for.

6. Mobile Optimization: Since most people see websites on their cell phones, make sure your website is mobile-friendly. Conversion rates may rise on a website optimized for mobile devices.

7. Social evidence: To gain the audience's confidence, provide them with social evidence in the form of industry recognition, security certifications, and trust badges.

8. Urgency and Scarcity: Instill a feeling of urgency and scarcity by presenting specials, discounts, or limited-edition items. This may entice users to click through on your affiliate links and buy something.

9. Unambiguous Call-to-Actions: To encourage visitors to click on your affiliate links, use call-to-actions (CTAs) that are both obvious and conspicuous. Use verbiage that encourages action, such as "Sign Up Today" or "Buy Now".

10. A/B Testing: Use A/B testing to test various website designs, content, and call-to-actions (CTAs) to see which ones your audience responds to the best.

You can improve your website's conversion rate and raise the likelihood that users will click on your affiliate links and complete a purchase by putting these tactics into practice.

Additional Tips

- Use analytics tools and heat maps to better analyze visitor behavior and adjust your website.

-Make use of exit-intent pop-ups to provide customers who are about to leave your website with last-minute deals or promotions.

- In return for visitors' email addresses, offer freebies or trials. This may assist grow your email list and boost conversion rates.

- To maximize your affiliate marketing efforts, *Use website optimization tools designed specifically for affiliate marketing, like WP Affiliate Manager or Affiliate Link Cloaker.

USING PAID ADVERTISING TO SUPERCHARGE YOUR AFFILIATE MARKETING

You may increase traffic, reach a larger audience, and increase conversions with the use of paid advertising. We'll go into the realm of paid advertising in this chapter and demonstrate how to utilize it to boost your affiliate marketing campaigns.

Let's start by discussing the advantages of sponsored advertising. Using sponsored advertisements, you can:

- Get your message in front of thousands of prospective buyers by reaching a large audience - Increase targeted traffic to your website or landing page

- Become more credible and raise brand recognition Measure your ROI and keep track of your outcomes.

Let's now explore the many kinds of sponsored advertising choices that are open to you. You possess:

- Facebook Ads: excellent for targeting particular interests, behaviors, and lookalike audiences

- Google Ads (formerly Google AdWords): ideal for targeting specific keywords and demographics

- Native Ads: blend in with the content of a website or platform for a more subtle approach

- Instagram Ads: visually appealing and ideal for promoting goods or services with strong visual appeal

- Twitter Ads: real-time targeting and engagement for promoting time-sensitive deals or trending

- LinkedIn Ads: perfect for B2B marketing and targeting professionals based on job title, industry, or firm

- YouTube Ads: reach a big audience with video-based advertising

Keep the following in mind when utilizing paid advertising for affiliate marketing:

Establish clear objectives and tracking: specify your campaign's aims and use tracking pixels to gauge its effectiveness. Select suitable ad platforms: pick ones that complement your target market and line of business.

- Create great ad creative by using attention-grabbing images, attention-grabbing headlines, and convincing language; - Optimize ad targeting by utilizing targeting choices to reach your targeted demographic and reduce waste.

- Track and fine-tune campaigns: For best outcomes, track performance, modify bids, and improve targeting.

- Adhere to affiliate marketing policies: Make sure you follow the rules and regulations about affiliate marketing set forth by the advertising platform.

- Clearly state that you are affiliated with the supplier of the product or service to maintain confidence and transparency.

These pointers can help you make the most money possible with affiliate marketing by increasing conversions, driving high-quality traffic, and using paid advertising wisely.

Additional Tips;

- AdPlexity and Affiliate Ad Rotator are paid advertising tools specifically designed for affiliate marketing.

- Use lookalike targeting to reach new audiences similar to your existing customers or website visitors.

- Use retargeting ads to reach users who have visited your website or engaged with your content.

- Take advantage of ad platform features like automated bidding, ad rotation, and A/B testing.

Recall that paid advertising is an effective way to expand your audience and increase revenue. You may succeed with affiliate marketing by implementing these suggestions and making efficient use of paid advertising.

CHAPTER 9

BUILDING A TEAM AND OUTSOURCING TASKS - BECAUSE YOU CAN'T DO IT ALONE!

Hello, fellow affiliate marketer! You're presumably feeling like a one-man army at this point, managing social media and creating content. The truth is, however, you don't have to do it by yourself! Putting together a team and contracting out work may completely transform your company.

When you attempt to handle everything on your own, you find that your time and knowledge are limited.

However, by assembling a group of specialists, you may make use of their knowledge and expertise to do more tasks faster. It's also much less stressful!

So how can you form a team and assign work to others? *The following advice will help you get started:*

- Determine your areas of weakness. Ask yourself honestly, what do you lack skill in? What eats up excessive amounts of your time? You need to delegate such chores to someone else first!

- Locate the proper people: Whether it's site design, social media management, or content development, seek out professionals in each area. To get assistance with administrative chores, you may employ a virtual assistant or look for freelancers on websites like Upwork or Fiverr.

-Make sure you are clear about what you need and when you need it.

- Communicate effectively. Establish due dates, provide instructions, and be accessible for inquiries.

- Trust and let go - You must trust your staff to do their duties, even if it might be difficult to relinquish control. Put your attention on important tasks and delegate the rest to your staff.

- Have patience - It takes time to assemble a team and outsource work, so don't expect results right away.

Among the common jobs that are outsourced are:

 - Content development (graphics, writing, and video production)

 - Management of social media (interaction, publishing, analytics)

 - Web development and design (creating and managing your website)

- Email marketing (automated newsletter generation)

- Virtual help (data input, administrative duties)

Creating a team and delegating work can free up more time for you to concentrate on high-level strategy and expansion.

Additional Tip;

- Start small: As you gain familiarity, progressively outsource additional work after starting with one or two.

- Clearly define your team's aims and objectives and make sure everyone is aware of what they are aiming for.

- Create a communication schedule. - Checking in often will help you keep informed about your progress.

- Be receptive to criticism and encourage your group to provide recommendations and thoughts.

-Express gratitude by praising and rewarding the efforts and accomplishments of your staff.

UNDERSTANDING AFFILIATE TRACKING AND ANALYTICS - THE SECRET TO MAXIMIZING YOUR EARNINGS!

Hello, fellow affiliate marketer! You may be wondering how to monitor your affiliate income and make data-driven choices to grow your company. Analytics and affiliate monitoring are essential for assessing your success, pinpointing problem areas, and fine-tuning your plan to maximize profits.

Consider affiliate analytics and monitoring to be similar to your company's GPS. It guides you through the affiliate marketing environment, helps you steer clear of expensive blunders, and gets you to your goal—maximum earnings!—faster.

Let's dissect it:

Tracking affiliates:

- The practice of tracking and documenting affiliate clicks, conversions, and referrals is known as affiliate tracking. It assists you in determining which marketing initiatives are generating the most revenue and which ones need development.

- You can improve your campaigns, find high-performing affiliates, and make well-informed choices about your marketing plan using affiliate monitoring.

Analytical:

- Analytics is the process of looking at data to find patterns and decide what to do.

Analytics in affiliate marketing aids in audience comprehension, performance monitoring, and pinpointing areas in need of development.

You can increase conversion rates, optimize your campaigns, and increase revenue with the help of analytics.

Several widely used tools for affiliate monitoring and analytics consist of:

- Google Analytics

- ClickMagick

- Pressure

- Affiliate Monitoring

- CPV Laboratory

Take into account the following factors when selecting an affiliate monitoring and analytics tool:

- Accuracy: Seek for instruments that provide precise reporting and tracking.

- Usability: Select instruments with intuitive user interfaces and easily comprehensible data.

- Customization: Choose solutions that let you adjust analytics and tracking to meet your specific requirements.

- Integration: Take into account solutions that work with the platforms and tools for marketing you already have.

Additional Tips;

-Start small: As you gain familiarity, progressively transition to more sophisticated technologies from basic monitoring and analytics.

- Specify your targets and utilize analytics to monitor your progress. - Establish specific goals.

Try new things and get the most out of your campaigns by using analytics to test new ideas and maximize results.

- Stay current: To guarantee reliable data and insights, keep your monitoring and analytics tools current.

Gaining proficiency in affiliate monitoring and analytics will enable you to improve your campaigns, make data-driven choices, and increase your revenue. Recall that information is power, and that data is king in affiliate marketing!

CHAPTER 10

THE KEY TO EXPLODING YOUR PROFITS: MAXIMIZING YOUR CAMPAIGN FOR MAXIMUM PROFIT

Now that your campaign is set up, you are beginning to notice some results. However, you're not quite achieving the desired profit margins. Rest assured, dear friend—optimization will help with that! We'll go into the details of campaign optimization for optimum profit in this chapter.

Optimizing a system is similar to tuning a high-performance vehicle. You've mastered the fundamentals, but you can make your campaign even better with a few little changes!

Now let's get going:

1. Monitor Your Metrics: Without measurement, it is impossible to optimize. Pay special attention to your KPIs, including profits per click, conversion rates, and click-through rates.

2. Find Your Best-Performing Resources: Which affiliate links, landing pages, and advertisements are generating the most revenue? Put forth much more effort on them!

3. Trim the Fat: Allocate your money to the winners and get rid of the underperforming assets.

4. Split testing: Determine which iterations of your affiliate links, landing pages, and advertisements work best by testing them all.

5. Optimize Your Landing Pages: Ensure that your landing pages are quick, easy to navigate, and conversion-focused.

6. Employ retargeting to connect with website visitors who have not yet completed a conversion.

7. Make use of email marketing: Create an email list and market to your audience with relevant offers.

8. Make Use of User-Generated Content: Invite clients to write about their interactions with your goods or services.

9. Keep Up with Industry Trends: Monitor news in the field and modify your approach as necessary.

10. Constantly Evaluate and Modify: The process of optimization is never-ending. To increase your earnings, keep an eye on your metrics and make any necessary improvements.

Additional Tip:

- Start small: Make little modifications at first, then work your way up.

- Have patience: The process of optimization requires work and patience.

- Remain organized: To make data-driven choices, keep track of your tests and outcomes.

- Don't be scared to attempt new things: Experimentation and trying out novel tactics are key components of optimization.

You may increase your profit margin and grow your affiliate marketing company by using these optimization techniques. Recall that optimization is a continuous process, and you may get amazing results if you have the correct attitude and resources!

AVOID AFFILIATE MARKETING MISTAKES - DON'T LET THESE COMMON PITFALLS HOLD YOU BACK!

It's simple to make errors while navigating the world of affiliate marketing, which may cost you credibility, money, and effort. But rest assured I got you covered! I have outline the most typical affiliate marketing blunders in this chapter and provide professional guidance on how to steer clear of them.

Error #1: Not Declaring Your Partnership

Solution: Be sure to always state that you are associated with the item or service you are endorsing. Openness is essential!

Error #2: Encouraging Products of Low Quality

Solution: Only endorse goods that live up to your standards and are consistent with your principles. It's what your reputation is all about!

Error #3: Not Establishing a Bond with Your Audience

Solution: Spend some time getting to know your audience and developing a rapport. It's more probable that they'll purchase from you!

Error #4: Not Monitoring Your Outcomes

Solution: Monitor your statistics and stats. Without measurement, optimization is impossible!

Error #5: Ignoring FTC Guidelines

Solution: Make sure you're following the most recent FTC requirements by keeping up with them.

Error #6: Improperly Dividing Your Revenue Sources

Remedy: Avoid putting all of your eggs in one basket! Spread out your sources of income to lower your risk.

Error #7: Lack of Patience

Answer: Affiliate marketing is not a sprint; it's a marathon. Be tenacious and patient!

Error #8: Not Adding Value

Solution: Pay attention to what your audience will benefit from. You'll get purchases and loyalty in return!

Error #9: Ignoring Email Marketing

Solution: Create an email list and market to your audience specifically.

Error #10: _Ignoring Current Trends in the Industry_

Solution: Keep up with the most recent developments in the sector and modify your plan as necessary.

These typical blunders may be avoided to help you develop an affiliate marketing company that succeeds, builds your internet profile, and makes steady earnings. Recall that affiliate marketing is a journey, and you may get amazing results if you have the correct attitude and tactics!

www.ingramcontent.com/pod-product-compliance
Lightning Source LLC
Chambersburg PA
CBHW050232230526
45470CB00005B/1911